DONATED BY
OAK RIDGE P.T.A.

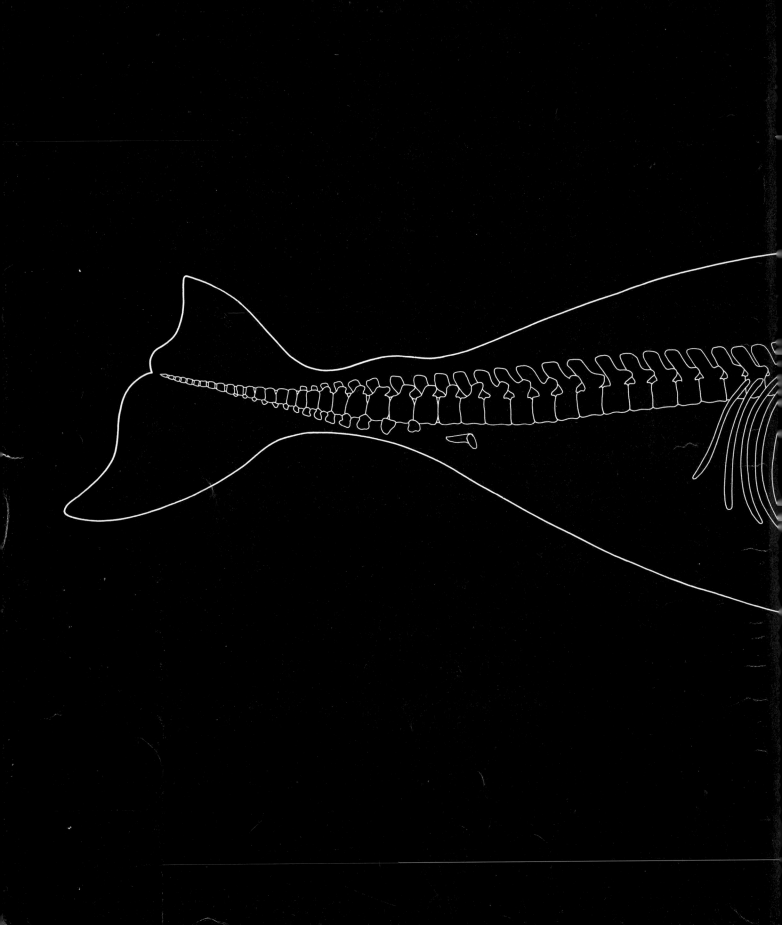

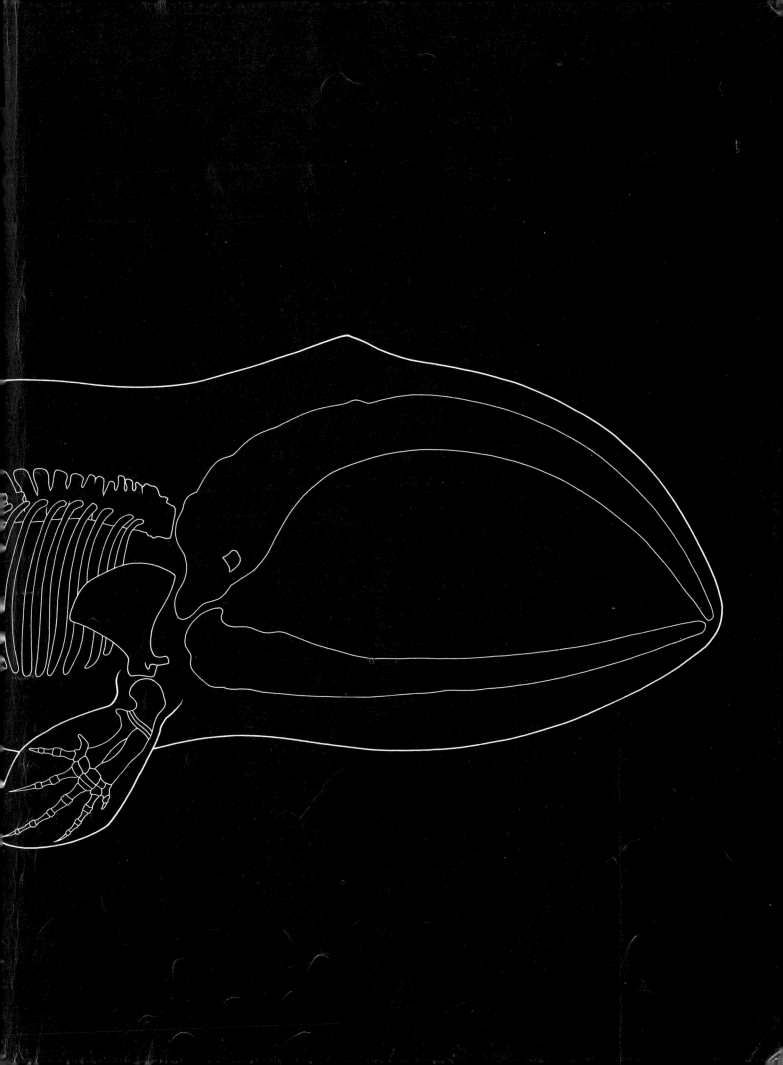

First published 1974
Macdonald and Co.
(Publishers) Limited
St Giles House
49–50 Poland Street
London W 1

© 1974 Macdonald and Co.
(Publishers) Limited

Adapted by M. L. McCarthy
*Editor*
Kate Woodhouse

*Assistant Editor*
Lesley Firth

*Designer*
Arthur Lockwood

*Illustrators*
Malcolm McGregor
Peter Connolly
Stephen Bennett
Ray Burrows
Corinne Clarke
Chris Howell-Jones

*Projects*
Gillian Lockwood

*Production*
Philip Hughes

Published in the United
States by Silver Burdett
Company, Morristown, N.J.
1979 Printing
Library of Congress
Catalog Card No. 78-56582
ISBN 0-382-06186-1

# The Life of
# Sea
# Mammals

Macdonald   Educational

# The Life of Sea Mammals

Life began in the sea,
millions of years ago.
Land animals come from
animals that came
out of the sea.
Some land animals
went back to the sea.
Whales were once
land animals.
They went back to the sea
about 45 million years ago.
Seals went back
about 20 million years ago.

Whales and seals
breathe air.
They are mammals.
They have babies, not eggs.
They feed their babies
on their own milk.

This book tells how
these animals
live in the sea.
It shows how
Eskimos hunt them.
It also shows how
whaling was done
a hundred years ago,
and how it is done today.

## Contents

### Reference and Projects

# How Sea Mammals Began

### What is a mammal?

1. A mammal is a warm blooded animal.

2. A mammal gives birth to live young.

3. A mammal feeds its young with milk.

4. A mammal breathes air.

5. A mammal is usually a four-footed animal covered with hair.

## About mammals

A mammal is an animal that feeds its babies with its own milk. Cats and dogs are mammals. Humans are mammals, too. Can you think of any other mammals?

Most mammals live on land. Some live in the sea, or spend much of the time in the sea. Whales and seals are sea mammals. So are sea cows and sea otters.

All mammals, and many other animals, breathe air.

Sea mammals breathe air, just like land mammals.

## Modern animals

Modern animals come from animals who lived millions of years ago. The first animals all lived in the sea. Later, some of them moved to the land. Once, all mammals lived on land. Some went back to sea. Perhaps they had enemies on land. Perhaps the sea had risen, and there was less land.

An animal called "creodont" lived on land 125 million years ago. It was the size of a rabbit, and ate meat. Many modern animals come from the creodont. Some live on land. Some live in the sea. This picture shows the mammals that come from the creodont.

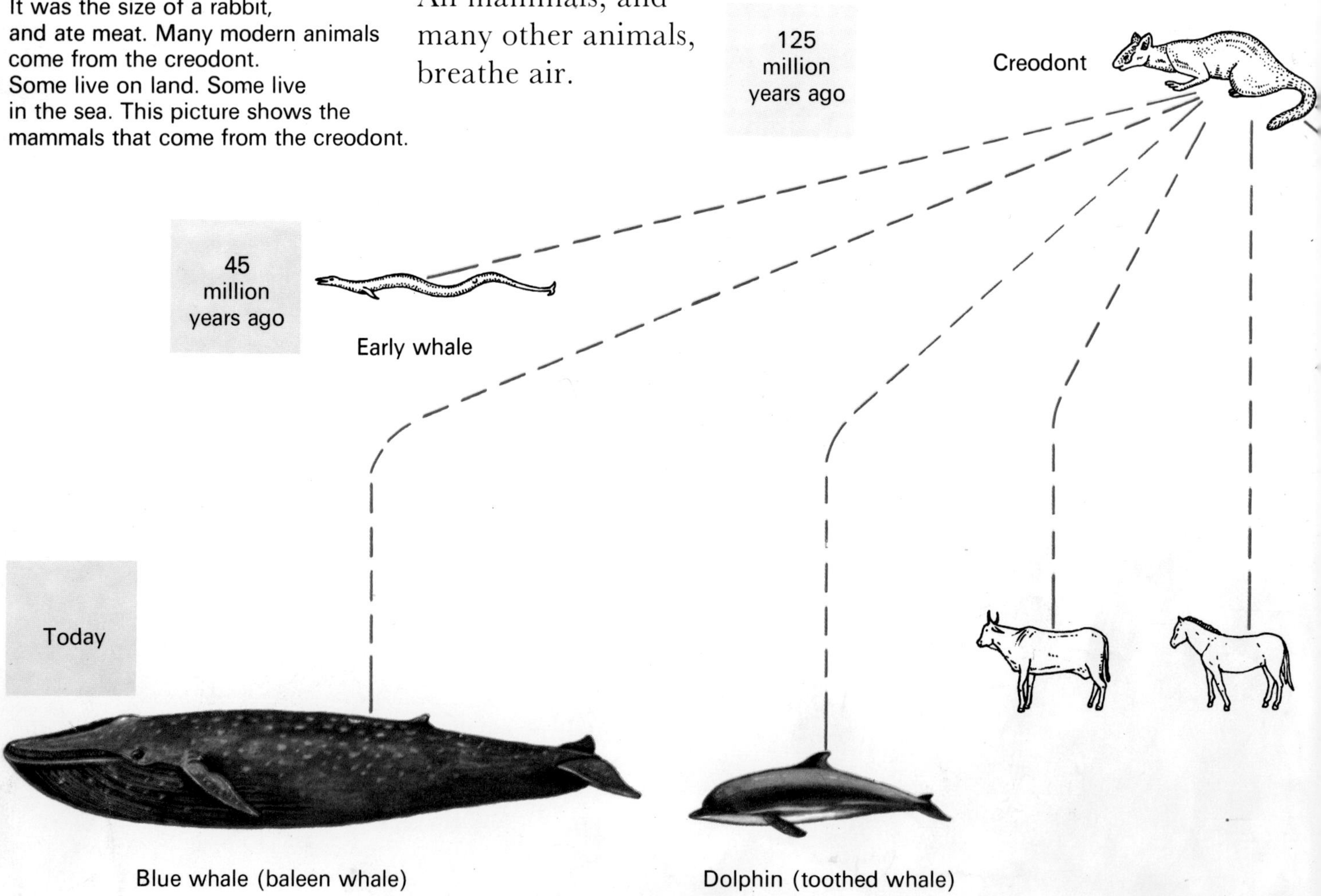

125 million years ago

Creodont

45 million years ago

Early whale

Today

Blue whale (baleen whale)

Dolphin (toothed whale)

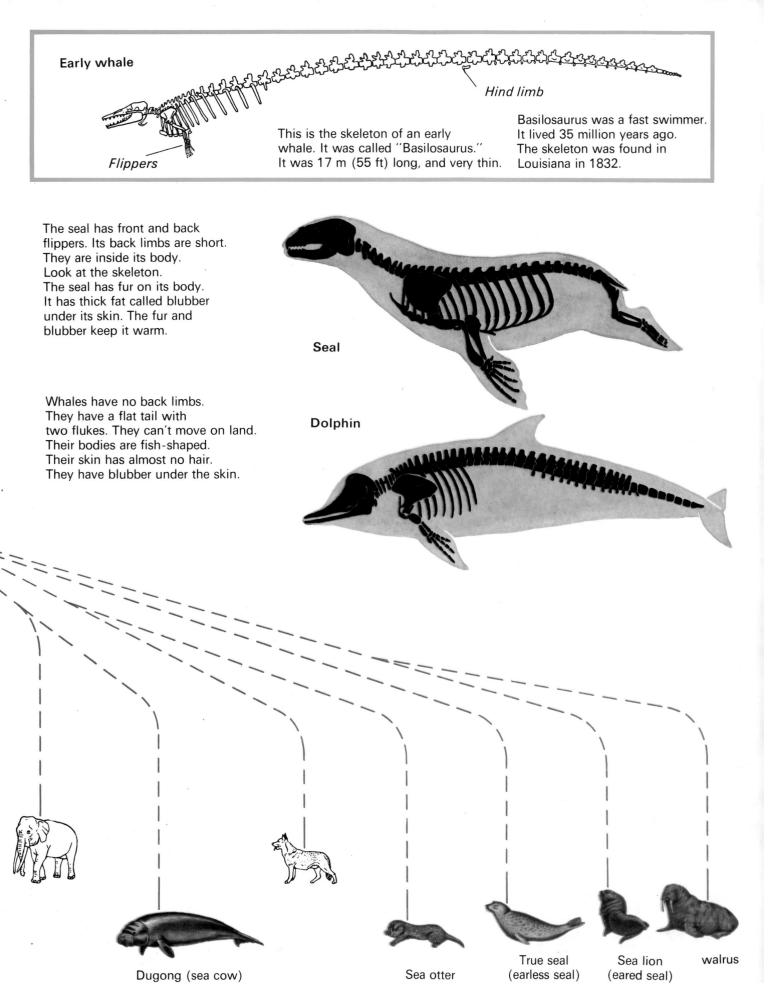

**Early whale**

*Hind limb*

*Flippers*

This is the skeleton of an early whale. It was called "Basilosaurus." It was 17 m (55 ft) long, and very thin.

Basilosaurus was a fast swimmer. It lived 35 million years ago. The skeleton was found in Louisiana in 1832.

The seal has front and back flippers. Its back limbs are short. They are inside its body. Look at the skeleton. The seal has fur on its body. It has thick fat called blubber under its skin. The fur and blubber keep it warm.

**Seal**

Whales have no back limbs. They have a flat tail with two flukes. They can't move on land. Their bodies are fish-shaped. Their skin has almost no hair. They have blubber under the skin.

**Dolphin**

Dugong (sea cow)

Sea otter

True seal (earless seal)

Sea lion (eared seal)

walrus

# Mating

Elephant seal

This elephant seal is a male.
He makes his nose very big
when he is angry.
The big nose makes him
look very fierce indeed !
He is fierce at mating time.
He roars at the other males,
and tries to drive them away
from the females.

Male (*bull*)

Female (*cow*)

Male sea lions are much bigger
than females. They have manes.
Spring is the time of mating.
Each male chooses his part
of the beach in springtime.
He drives all other males away.
Many females mate with him,
and have pups from this.

Many female elephant seals
mate with one strong male.
These seals lie on their sides
when they mate. They mate in winter.
The females are smaller than the males.

## Partners and groups

All mammals have babies
by the union
of females with males.
This is called "mating."

Sea mammals mate,
like all other mammals.

Whales cannot go on land.
They mate in the water.

Some seals and sea lions
mate on land.
Many male seals
fight with each other
at mating time.
Big males drive
smaller males away.
The females do not seem
to mind this.
Many females mate
with the same male.

Some seals mate in pairs.
They mate in the water.
The males do not fight
with each other.

Gray whales swim side by side when they mate. They do this in shallow water near the shore.

They stroke each other with their flippers and tails, and roll over one another.

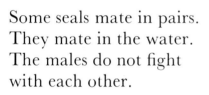

Humpback whales swim toward each other very fast. Then they press their bodies together and leap out of the water. It makes a great splash when they fall back into the water.

11

# Having Babies

A dolphin is a kind of whale.
This dolphin is having her baby.
The baby's tail comes out first.

The dolphin pushes her baby
to the top of the sea, so that it
can get air to breathe.
Another dolphin helps her.
Dolphins are helpful animals.

The pictures show how
fast a young blue whale
grows in its first 25 years.

## Pups and calves

A baby seal is called
a "pup."
Seal pups are born on land,
or on big pieces
of floating ice
called "ice floes."
Seal pups can swim
soon after they are born.

A baby whale is called
a "calf."
Whale calves are born
in the water.
They are born tail first.
They need to breathe air
at once.
Whale calves can swim
when they are born.
They swim to the top
of the water for air.

Most sea mammals
have only one baby
at a time.
Some have twins.

### Growth of a blue whale

When born:  length 7.3m (24 ft),
weight 2540 kg (25 tons).

Calf leaves its mother: length 16m
(53 ft), weight 23,370 kg (23 tons).

Five years old: length 23m (76 ft),
weight 81,285 kg (80 tons).

Twenty-five years old: length 25.5m
(84 ft), weight 111,7666 kg (110 tons).

This ringed seal has made a lair
for her baby under the snow.
She comes into it from the water.
Look at the hole in the water!
There are many ringed seals
in the Arctic region.

These seals are gray seals.
A female seal is called a "cow."
A male is called a "bull."
Males fight with one another
at mating time. Big bulls
drive off the smaller bulls.

Many bulls do not mate
because of this. A piece of beach
with a bull and cows and pups
is called a "rookery."
Small males gather at the edges
of the rookery. Sometimes
they fight with each other.

# Growing Up

This harp seal lies on the ice
and feeds her pup with her milk.
The pup drinks milk for two weeks.
Then it learns to catch food.
The mother eats very little
while she is suckling the pup.

There are hundreds of seals
in a colony. This kind of seal
is called a Pribilof fur seal.
Each mother knows the smell
of her own pup. She will not feed
any other pup except her own.
The seals hunt in the sea.
Each seal comes on land once
a week to feed her pup.

Male

Pup

Female

## Early life

The milk of a sea mammal
is very rich.
Baby sea mammals
grow very fast
on this rich food.

There are many
dangerous animals
that would like to eat
the baby sea mammal.
There are storms at sea,
and the babies can't swim
in the rough water.
Baby sea mammals can die
of sicknesses that
would not hurt a grown-up.
Big seals sometimes lie
on their pups,
and hurt them
without meaning it.

Many baby sea mammals
have to grow quickly.
If they do not
grow quickly,
very few of them
would live to grow up.
There would soon
be no more sea mammals.

This whale is feeding
her calf under the water,
by squirting milk
into the calf's mouth.
The calf does not
have to suck.

This sea otter is carrying her pup.
She looks after it until it is
one year old. She teaches it
to catch shellfish, and break
the shells on a stone.
Sea otters live in shallow water.

Ear plug

### Telling the age

The dark rings
on a whale's ear plug
and on its teeth
show the whale's age.

Sperm whale's tooth

# How Whales Eat

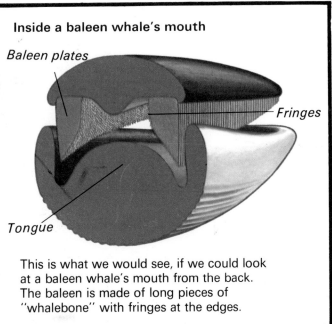

**Inside a baleen whale's mouth**

*Baleen plates*

*Fringes*

*Tongue*

This is what we would see, if we could look at a baleen whale's mouth from the back. The baleen is made of long pieces of "whalebone" with fringes at the edges.

Many of the biggest whales have a baleen instead of teeth. The whale in this picture is a Southern Right whale. Right whales have very long baleen plates.

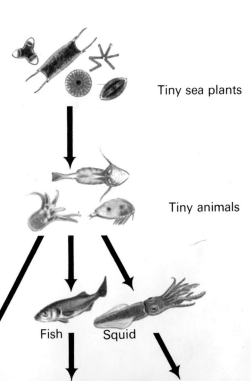

Tiny sea plants

Tiny animals

Fish    Squid

Krill (real size)

Krill eat small sea plants. Baleen whales eat *them*. Fish and squid also eat krill. Whales that have teeth eat fish and squid.

Greenland Right whale

Sperm whale

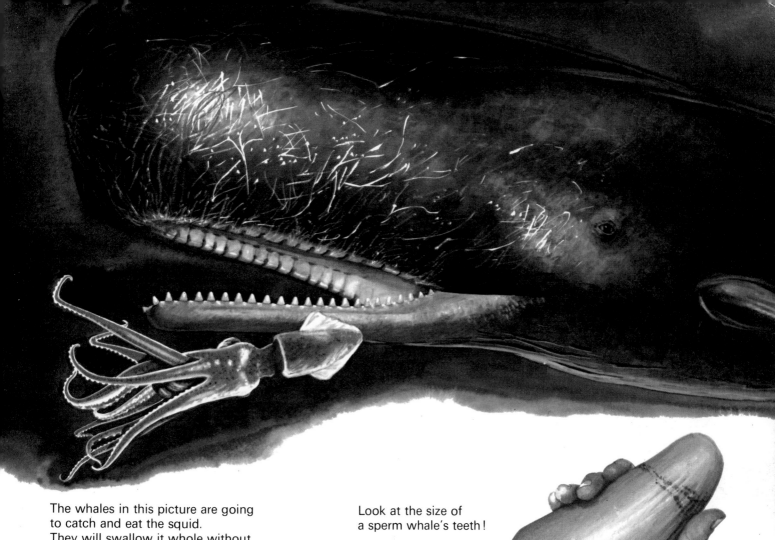

The whales in this picture are going to catch and eat the squid. They will swallow it whole without chewing. Squid are about 0.6-2 m (2-6 ft) long. Some are 10.5 m (34.5 ft) long! Sperm whales also eat fish, but like squid better.

Look at the size of a sperm whale's teeth!

## Swallowing food whole

Some whales eat shrimps and other small animals. These are the biggest whales. They have no teeth. Instead they have a grid called a "baleen."

The baleen hangs from the top of the mouth. The whale takes water into its mouth, and when it closes its mouth, its tongue pushes the water out again.

Small animals in the water are caught on the baleen.

Some whales eat fish. Others eat squid. All these whales have teeth.

Whales with teeth do not chew their prey. They swallow them whole. No one knows why they have teeth. Most whales with teeth are smaller than whales with a baleen.

This whale has teeth. It is a dolphin.

17

# Meat Eaters and Plant Eaters

The crabeater seal lives by the South Pole. It eats krill, not crabs. It has prongs on its teeth. It catches the krill just as a baleen whale does.

The walrus eats shellfish. It digs them up with its long tusks. Then it sucks the shellfish from the shell and swallows them.

The leopard seal is a very fierce hunter. It catches fish and squid. It also hunts sea birds, and it eats the pups of other kinds of seals. This one has killed a penguin. It will eat the flesh and throw the skin away.

## Seals eat fish

Seals have teeth.
Many seals
eat fish and squid.
They do not use
their teeth
to chew the food.
They use them for
holding it and tearing it.

Seals swallow
small fish whole.
They tear big fish up,
and swallow the pieces.

Some seals hunt sea birds,
or baby sea mammals.
Some seals eat
shrimps and crabs
and shellfish.

Seals can live for weeks
without eating at all.
They don't eat when
their babies are small.
They live on their body fat.

Manatees are useful to humans.
They eat plants that would block
rivers. They like eating.

Sea cows live in shallow water.
They live in the mouths of rivers.
They also live in shallow water
near the coast. They live in
warm parts of the world.
They have thick blubber. There
is almost no hair on their skin.
Their tails are flat.
Sea cows eat only water plants.
One kind of sea cow is
called a "manatee," and another
kind is called a "dugong."

Dugongs live in groups.
They like quiet, shallow water.
They are very gentle.

19

# Hunting

The grampus is a fierce, clever whale.
It hunts seals and dolphins. These
seals are twisting and turning
to get away from the grampus.
If they do get away, the grampus
will starve. The grampus is often
called the "killer whale."

## Enemies

If a big whale is attacked,
it hits the enemy
with its tail.
A whale with teeth
will also snap and bite.

Dolphins are not
very big whales,
but they move very fast.
They hit an enemy
with their beaks,
and lash the water
with their tails.

Sharks and killer whales
kill whale calves
and seal pups.
So do leopard seals.
They also hunt
grown-up seals.

Big seals bite and snap
at an enemy.
It is best for a seal
to swim away from
a big, fierce hunter.
Seals can twist and turn
very fast,
to tire their enemies.

Dolphins are very clever whales.
They can drive a shark away.
They hit it with their beaks, and
lash the water with their tails.
The shark can't see, and can't
swim straight. Dolphins sometimes
drive hungry sharks away from
whales that are having babies.

Walrus live by the North Pole.
Sometimes polar bears attack
walrus pups, and the mother walrus
hits at the bears with her tusks.

Many killer whales may attack
and eat a very big whale.
A killer whale may eat more than
twenty seals, one after the other.

This polar bear hopes that the seal
will come out of the water.
Seals can swim faster than bears,
but they move slowly on land.

21

# Traveling

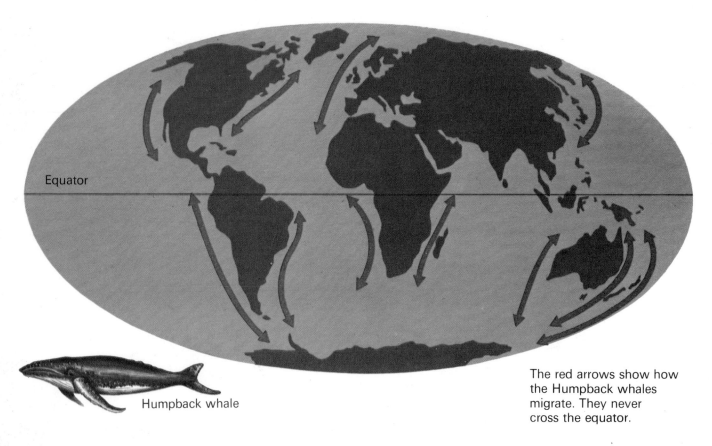

Equator

Humpback whale

The red arrows show how the Humpback whales migrate. They never cross the equator.

## Long journeys

Some humpback whales
live north of the equator.
Some live south of it.

The humpback whales
in the south
go toward the South Pole
in the summer.
They go toward
the equator in winter.

The whales in the north
go toward the North Pole
in summer.
They go toward
the equator in winter.

Many other big whales
also move to colder parts
in the summer,
and warmer parts in winter.

This kind of travel
is called "migration."

Some land animals migrate.
Some birds migrate.

When birds migrate,
the flock moves
in a V-shape.
Watch for this in autumn.

Seals feed at sea

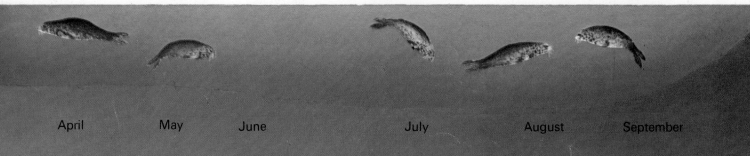

April          May          June                    July          August          September

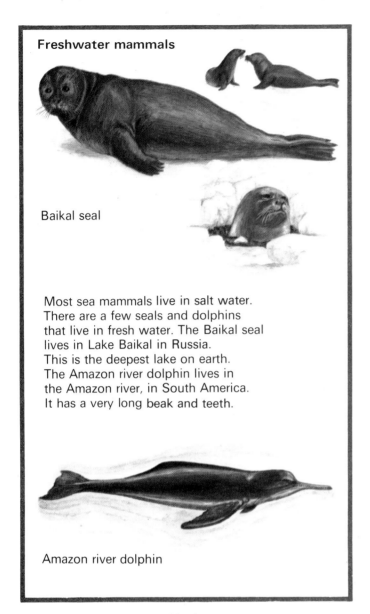

## Freshwater mammals

Baikal seal

Most sea mammals live in salt water.
There are a few seals and dolphins
that live in fresh water. The Baikal seal
lives in Lake Baikal in Russia.
This is the deepest lake on earth.
The Amazon river dolphin lives in
the Amazon river, in South America.
It has a very long beak and teeth.

Amazon river dolphin

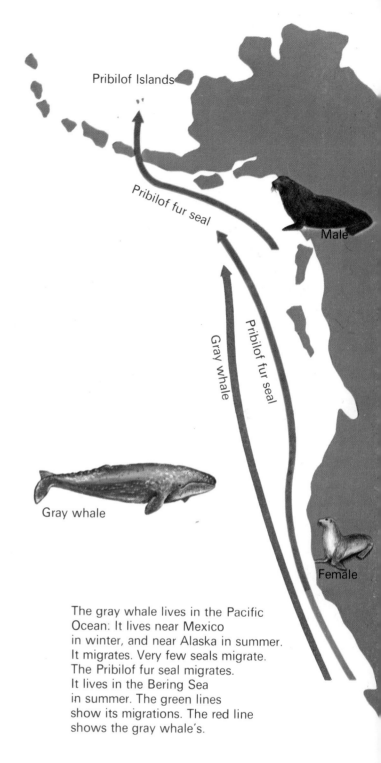

Pribilof Islands

Pribilof fur seal

Male

Gray whale

Pribilof fur seal

Gray whale

Female

The gray seal lives in the North
Atlantic Ocean. The pictures below
show how gray seals spend the year.
A gray seal has her baby one year
after mating.
She mates again two weeks
after having the baby.
Gray seals feed at sea all summer.
They molt on land in spring.

The gray whale lives in the Pacific
Ocean: It lives near Mexico
in winter, and near Alaska in summer.
It migrates. Very few seals migrate.
The Pribilof fur seal migrates.
It lives in the Bering Sea
in summer. The green lines
show its migrations. The red line
shows the gray whale's.

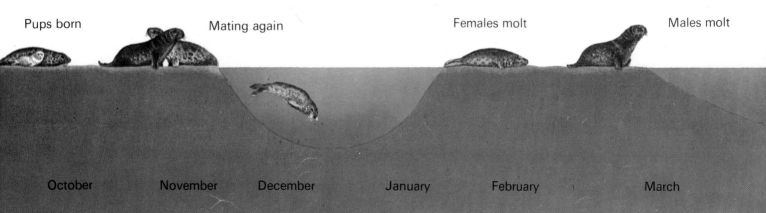

Pups born     Mating again        Females molt     Males molt

October     November     December     January     February     March

# Swimming and Walking

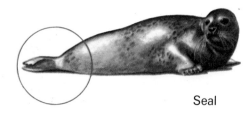

Seal

Seals cannot move well on land.
They can't turn their back
flippers. They drag themselves
along. The front flippers take
all their weight.
Sea lions move fast on land.
Their back flippers can turn
forward, and allow them to walk
and even run.

Sea lion

### Adapting

A whale's body is wide
at the front,
and narrow at the tail.
It is very smooth, because
the whale has blubber
under its skin.
It moves easily
through the water.

Whales have flat tails
with big tail flukes.
Instead of arms,
they have flippers.
Some whales have
a fin on their backs.

Seals have furry flippers.
They swim by moving
their back flippers
from side to side.
The front flippers
stay flat against the body.

Sea lions have flippers
with no fur on them.
They use their
front flippers for swimming.
They steer with
their back flippers.

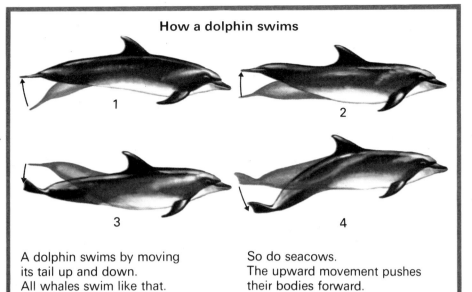

## How a dolphin swims

1

2

3

4

A dolphin swims by moving
its tail up and down.
All whales swim like that.

So do seacows.
The upward movement pushes
their bodies forward.

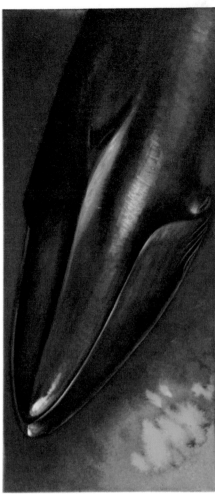

Look at the two nostrils,
in a V-shape on the top
of this sei whale's head.

The whale's snout is long, and it
becomes narrower towards the front.
A whale's body is shaped like
a torpedo. It moves easily and
quickly through the water.

The Humpback whale is very playful.
It loves to knock the water about.
It hits the water with its tail and flippers.
Sometimes it jumps out of the sea,
and falls back with a great splash.

# Breathing and Diving

*Nostrils open*

A seal's nostrils are on the end
of its snout, like a cat's or a dog's.
The nostrils are kept closed,
when the head is under water.
The seal would die,
if water filled its lungs.

A whale breathes through
an opening called a "blowhole."
The blowhole is kept closed
when the head is under water.
This minke whale has two
nostrils at its blowhole.

*Nostrils closed*

## Breathing air

Sea mammals have lungs,
just like land mammals.
They cannot breathe in
oxygen from the water
like fish.
They take oxygen
from the air,
as cats, dogs, and humans do.

Sea mammals dive for food.
A sea mammal
takes a big breath
before it dives.
Most dives last
only a few minutes.

A seal can stay
under the water
for about half-an-hour.

Sperm whales can stay under
water  for an hour.

A sea mammal breathes out
when it has finished
its dive.
Then it breathes in new air.
It can empty its lungs,
and fill them again,
all in one breath.
Land mammals can't do that.

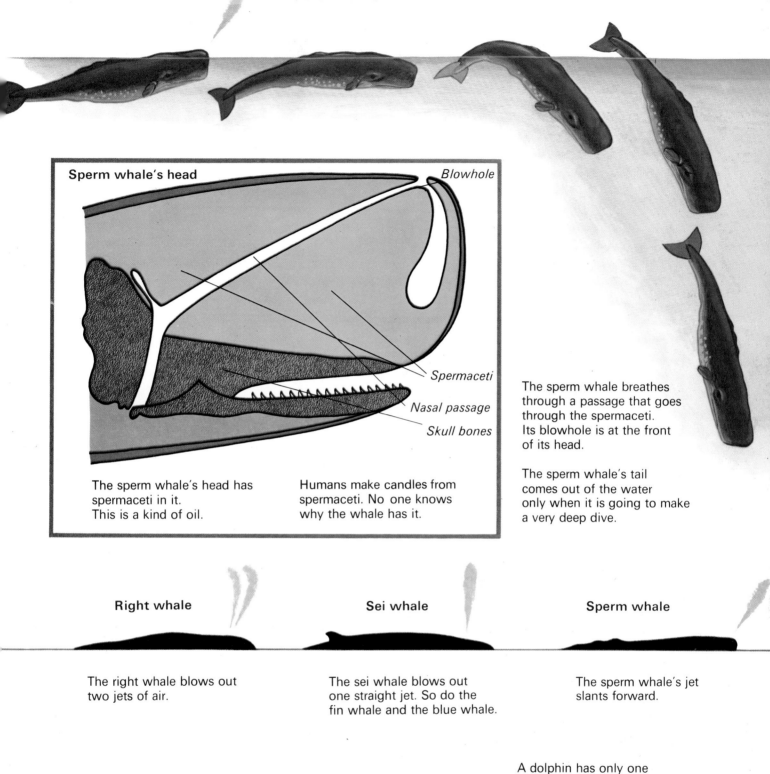

**Sperm whale's head**

*Blowhole*

*Spermaceti*

*Nasal passage*

*Skull bones*

The sperm whale's head has spermaceti in it. This is a kind of oil.

Humans make candles from spermaceti. No one knows why the whale has it.

The sperm whale breathes through a passage that goes through the spermaceti. Its blowhole is at the front of its head.

The sperm whale's tail comes out of the water only when it is going to make a very deep dive.

**Right whale**

The right whale blows out two jets of air.

**Sei whale**

The sei whale blows out one straight jet. So do the fin whale and the blue whale.

**Sperm whale**

The sperm whale's jet slants forward.

A dolphin has only one opening to its blowhole.

# Fur, Skin, and Blubber

The banded seal lives in the North Pacific Ocean. The seals in the picture are males. They are lying on an ice floe.
Male banded seals have yellow bands on their fur.
Females are pale brown.
Small pups are white.

This is a harp seal pup.
It has a white woolly coat when it is very small.
Older pups have a gray coat.

*Guard hairs*

*Soft hairs*

*Skin*

**Seal's fur**

Seals and sea lions have soft, thick hairs next to the skin. They also have very long, stiff "guard hairs."
These are longer than the soft hairs, and stick out beyond them.

This dying whale has been
washed up onto the beach.
Whales cannot move at all
on land.
The sun dries their thin skin.
The whale's body is made
for life in the water.

## Keeping warm

Seals and sea lions
have hairy coats.
Their coats keep them
warm and dry,
even under water
They molt in spring
just like cats and dogs.
Then they grow new fur.

They have oily skin.
Salt water doesn't hurt it.
They have thick blubber
under their skin.
This keeps them warm.

Whales have almost no hair
on their bodies.
They have only
a few bristles on their heads.
They have thick blubber
under their skin,
just as seals have.

The blubber keeps
them warm.
Since whales never leave
the sea they can live for
weeks on their blubber
without eating.

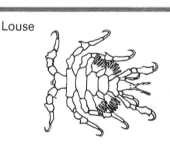

Louse

Lice live on some whales.
They hide in folds of the
whale's skin.
They cling to the skin
with their sharp claws.
Some whales have barnacles
fixed to their skin.
Barnacles sometimes grow
on a whale's broken tooth.

Barnacles

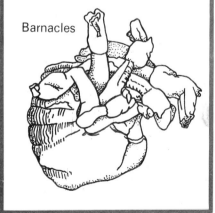

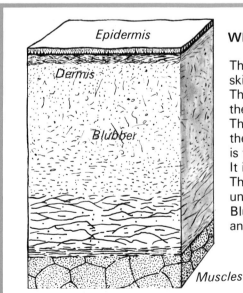

Epidermis

Dermis

Blubber

Muscles

### Whale skin

The top layer of a whale's
skin is very thin.
This top layer is called
the "epidermis."
The layer below
the epidermis
is thicker.
It is called the "dermis."
The blubber is
under the dermis.
Blubber is very thick
and very tough.

# Echoes and Talking

**Echo sounding**

This ship is sending down
pings of sound into
the sea. The sounds
bounce back to the ship.
The people in the ship
find out the shape of
the sea bed from the echo.

This white whale is called
a beluga. It makes whistling
sounds under the water.
People can hear these whistles
above the water.

No one knows how the beluga makes
these whistling sounds.
Scientists think that air moves
about in the beluga's head
and in its throat.

**Finding a fish by echo**

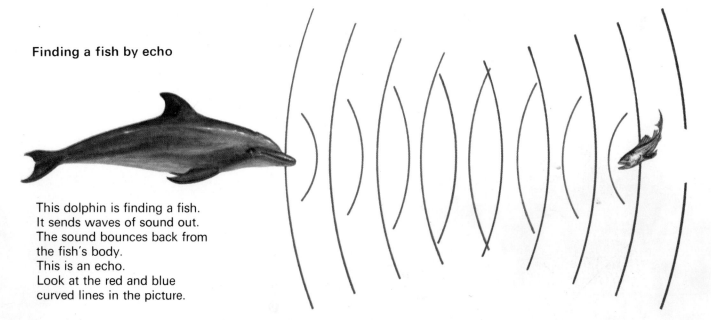

This dolphin is finding a fish.
It sends waves of sound out.
The sound bounces back from
the fish's body.
This is an echo.
Look at the red and blue
curved lines in the picture.

These two male
elephant seals are very
angry with each other.
They show it by rearing up,
and roaring loudly in
each other's face.
This noise says, "Go away!
This isn't your beach!
It's mine!"

## Sea sounds

All animals "tell" things
to each other.
They do this
by making noises.
They also do this
by the way they move,
and by touching each other.
Watch two cats or dogs.

Whales make noises
to tell each other things.
They "speak" to each other
under the water.
Scientists don't know
how whales
make these noises, but
they think the sounds are
made inside their heads.

Seals and sea lions
tell things to each other
by the way they move.
They also make sounds
when they are on land.
They make these sounds
just as land animals do.
They also sniff
and touch each other.

Dolphins whistle under water.
They also make clicking sounds.
They send out clicks to make echoes.
Two dolphins in the same tank
make whistles and clicks together,
as if they were talking.

Scientists make records of the
noises that tame dolphins make
to each other.
It is very difficult to find out
if they are "talking"
or only making sounds.

Clicking dolphin

Whistling dolphin

# Senses

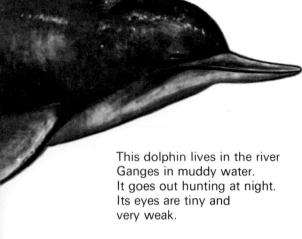

This dolphin lives in the river
Ganges in muddy water.
It goes out hunting at night.
Its eyes are tiny and
very weak.

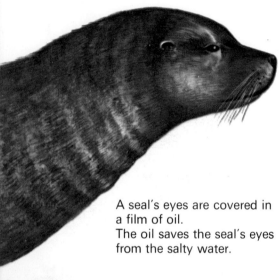

A seal's eyes are covered in
a film of oil.
The oil saves the seal's eyes
from the salty water.

Seals and sea lions have thick
whiskers for touching and feeling.
A walrus is a sea lion.
It has very long, stiff whiskers.
It digs up foods with its tusks,
and feels the food
with its whiskers before eating.

Whales have rather small eyes.
They see quite well. There is
light at the top of the sea.
The deep sea is very dark.

**Inside a whale's ear**

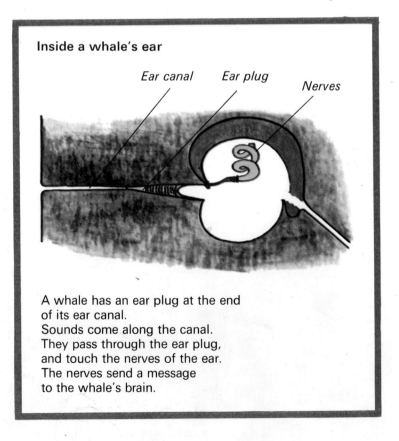

*Ear canal*  *Ear plug*  *Nerves*

A whale has an ear plug at the end
of its ear canal.
Sounds come along the canal.
They pass through the ear plug,
and touch the nerves of the ear.
The nerves send a message
to the whale's brain.

## Eyes and ears

Whales hear very well.
So do seals and sea lions.
They can find food,
or find their way about,
by sending out sounds
and listening for the echo.

Seals have big eyes.
They see very well,
both in water and in air.
There is a film of oil
over a seal's eyes
to protect them from
the salty water.

Whales have small eyes,
but they see quite well.

Whales can't smell much.
Sea cows smell very well.
So do seals and sea lions.

Whales like to touch things.
Seals also have
a good sense of touch.
All sea mammals
have a sense of taste.

A human's eye under water

The human eye has a
disc-shaped lens for
seeing in the air.
It is farsighted
under water,
because light
isn't fixed on the
back of the eye.

*Lens*

A dolphin's eye under water

A whale's eye has a
round lens for
seeing in the water.
Rays of light are
fixed onto the back
of the eye.
The back is the part
that sees.

*Lens*

A dolphin's eye out of water

A whale's eye is
nearsighted in air.
The round lens
can't carry the
rays of light
to the back
of the eye.

*Lens*

This gray whale is "spy-hopping."
It is standing up in the water,
and looking around to see
what is going on up above.
The minke whale and the
killer whale also spy-hop.
These whales must see well in air,
or they would not do this.
Tame dolphins can catch fish,
and play games in the air.

# Tame Sea Mammals

## A dolphin helps scientists

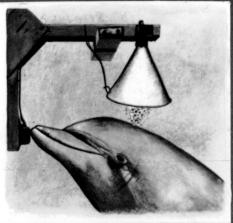

Scientists have taught this clever tame dolphin to dive down to the bottom of the tank, and blow air into a funnel. The scientists study this air from the dolphin's lungs, so that they may help human divers.

Tame dolphins show off, leaping from the water, all together. Humans love to watch this! Wild dolphins also play games with each other. Dolphins like other dolphins. They also like humans.

## Teaching dolphins

Whales are very clever.
Humans can teach them
to play games,
and do jobs for them.

Seals and sea lions
are clever, too.
Humans can teach them tricks
and games.
You may have seen
sea lions at a zoo
playing with a ball.
They toss the ball
to each other.

These clever sea mammals
like being with humans
and learning from them.

Wild sea mammals
won't eat dead fish.
The trainer teaches
the tame sea mammal
to eat dead, fresh fish.
When the animal
learns a new game,
the trainer is pleased,
and gives it a fish.

Humans keep tame killer whales,
as well as dolphins.
This big, clever whale loves games.
Humans can't keep the very biggest
whales as pets, because
they need so much water.

Whales learn to do jobs,
as well as to play games.
This whale has found a torpedo
on the bed of the sea.
She will lift it to the top.
Whales also help human divers,
and bring tools down to them.

# By the South Pole

## Cold climate mammals

Many sea mammals
live near the South Pole.
There are leopard seals,
who chase penguins
in the sea,
or catch them on the ice.
They also eat seal pups.

There are very many
crabeater seals.
They eat shrimps, not crabs.

Weddell seals swim
under the ice to hunt fish.
The ross seal
feeds mostly on squid.

The picture on the right
shows these animals
as they chase their prey.

The picture also shows
the blue whale.
The blue whale
is the biggest animal
ever known on earth.
It is a baleen whale and
it eats shrimps and krill.
It is in danger
of dying out because
it has been hunted so much.

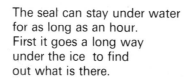

This Weddell seal is hunting
fish under the ice.
It finds a thin place in
the ice, and makes a hole.
It goes into the sea
through this hole,
and comes back to it
for air
from time to time.

The seal can stay under water
for as long as an hour.
First it goes a long way
under the ice  to find
out what is there.

Then it makes a deep dive
to find fish. It always finds
the hole again, even at night.
Scientists think that the seal
sends out sounds, and finds
the hole by the echo.

Skua

Fulmar

Crabeater seal

Emperor penguin

Adelie penguins

Leopard seal

Weddell seal

Ross seal

Blue whale

South America

South Pole

Krill

The little picture on the left shows the land around the South Pole. This land is called Antarctica. The land at the top left of the picture is South America. Antarctica is very cold.

No humans live on it. There is ice all around the land and in the sea. Plants don't grow in Antarctica. Birds and sea mammals live around the coast. See the picture above. The red in the little picture shows where the Weddell seal lives.

# Eskimo Hunters

Eskimo hunters wait for hours
by a seal's breathing hole, until
the seal comes up for air.
They kill the seal with a spear.
The spear is called a "harpoon."

Eskimos have boats called "kayaks."
They hunt whales from them.
Many kayaks come round the whale.
The hunters stab it with harpoons.
The whale-meat makes a feast
for everyone in the village.

## Arctic life

Eskimos live
in the ice deserts
near the North Pole.
Their lives are hard.

Almost no plants grow
in such places as
Greenland. Since
Eskimos can't be farmers,
they must be hunters.

There are not many
land animals
in the ice desert.
Eskimos catch fish
and hunt sea mammals.
They must make everything
that they need to live,
from the animals they kill.

Eskimos make
their weapons and tools
from the bones of whales.
They make their clothes
from the skins of seals.
Their sledges and boats
are also made from bones
and skins.
Every bit of the kill
has some use.

This Eskimo is cooking whale-meat.
The fire on which she cooks it is
from whale's oil.
Her clothes are made of sealskin.
They were sewn with bone needles,
and thread made of sinews.
She has no cloth, no steel, no wood.

# Hunting Long Ago

## Uses of sea mammals

Humans have always hunted
sea mammals.
They shot seals,
or clubbed them.
They caught whales
by throwing harpoons at them.
They wanted blubber,
for lamps or for cooking.
The meat of many
sea mammals is
good to eat.

Clothes and shoes
are made from the skins
of seals, sea otters,
and walrus.

Hunters shot walruses for their
meat, skin, and ivory tusks.
They were easy to hunt because
they are slow movers. They like
lying in the sun on ice floes.

Right whales were hunted
for the long pieces
of their baleen.
The baleen was called
"whalebone."
Whalebone was made
into stays for corsets,
and into spokes
for umbrellas.

Spermaceti comes from
the sperm whale's head.
It was made
into candles.

Japanese hunters caught whales in nets.
They threw the nets from small boats.

Humans used to hunt whales
from little wooden boats.
They threw harpoons at them.
The whales hit the boats with
their tails and often knocked
them over.

41

# Modern Hunting

### Killing seals

Fur seals are killed for their fur. Soap is made from the blubber. Hens eat the meat. The seals are killed very quickly with a club. Hunters kill mostly males.

These men live in the Faeroe Islands. They drive pilot whales into the shore and kill them. They want their oil and meat.

## Modern methods

Modern hunters kill whales
with explosive harpoons.
They hunt whales
from fast little boats
called "catcher boats."
Even the fastest whales
can't get away.

The most important thing
from a dead whale
is its oil.
This is used in industry.

Humans and animals
eat whale meat.
The bones are ground
into bone meal.
This is put into gardens
to feed the vegetables.

The head of a modern harpoon
has a grenade in it. The grenade
explodes inside the whale
and kills it at once.
The catcher boat drags the body
back to a big factory ship.
It is cut up on the ship.

### Harpoon heads

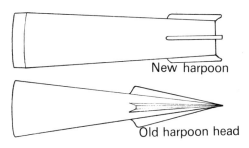

New harpoon

Old harpoon head

### The factory ship

Look at the numbers, in the
picture on the left.

1. The stern slipway to haul whales.

2. The deck on which
   the blubber is cut off.

3. The winches and cables
   to drag the whale
   up the slipway.

4. The deck on which
   the bones and meat are cut up.

5. The openings
   of great cookers under the deck.
   The cooking draws out the oil.

6. The hull of the ship.
   It has cookers, and storage tanks,
   and cabins for the crew.

7. A catcher boat.

43

# Stories and Pictures

This painting of dolphins,
fish, and sea plants,
was made about 4,000 years ago.
It is in the Palace of Knossus,
on the island of Crete.
It is painted on a wall.

The Bible tells the story of Jonah.
Some bad people threw him into
the sea. A big "fish" swallowed him.
It threw him onto the shore,
after three days and three nights.
The "fish" may have been a whale.

This old Greek coin shows
a boy riding on a dolphin.
In 1955, a dolphin played
with people swimming
near Opononi in New Zealand.
She took them for rides
on her back!

Everyone has heard of mermaids.
They sit on rocks in the sea, and sing
to the sailors who pass by. Really,
the sailors saw seals and sea cows.
They heard the seals' high wailing.
They were lonely for their wives,
and dreaming did the rest!

## Fact and fiction

Early humans lived in caves.
They drew pictures
of many animals
on the walls of the caves.
Some of these pictures
are of dolphins
and other whales.

The Maori people
of New Zealand
thought dolphins were gods.
Sailors told tall stories
about very big whales that
were mistaken for islands.

There are many Greek
and Roman stories
about friendly dolphins.
They saved people who
had fallen into the sea.

There are old stories
from Northwest Europe
about whales as monsters,
with scales like fish.
They were said to attack
every ship that they saw.
In truth, whales only
attacked whaling ships.

This is a "scrimshaw" picture.
It was scratched with a needle
on the tooth of a sperm whale.
Lampblack was rubbed into
the scratches to make them show
up. Then the tooth was polished.
There are teeth with scrimshaw
in most whaling museums.

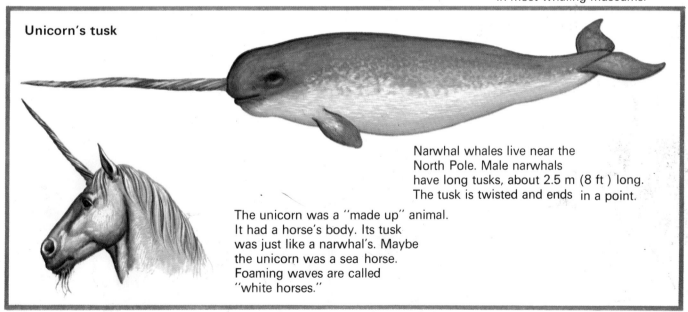

**Unicorn's tusk**

Narwhal whales live near the
North Pole. Male narwhals
have long tusks, about 2.5 m (8 ft) long.
The tusk is twisted and ends in a point.

The unicorn was a "made up" animal.
It had a horse's body. Its tusk
was just like a narwhal's. Maybe
the unicorn was a sea horse.
Foaming waves are called
"white horses."

# The Whale Family

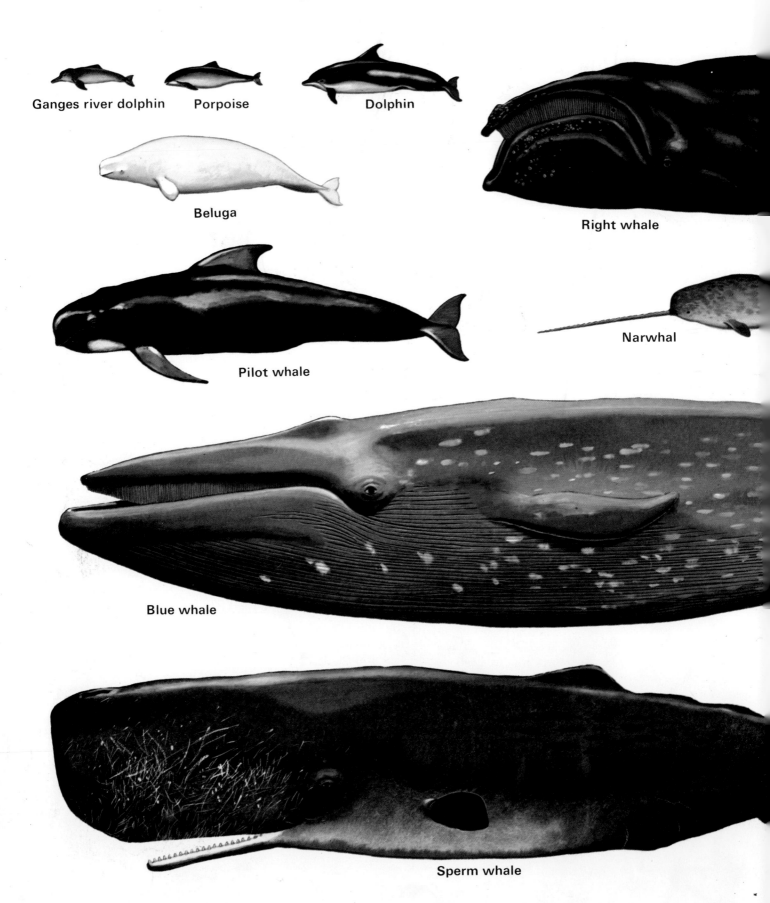

Ganges river dolphin

Porpoise

Dolphin

Beluga

Right whale

Pilot whale

Narwhal

Blue whale

Sperm whale

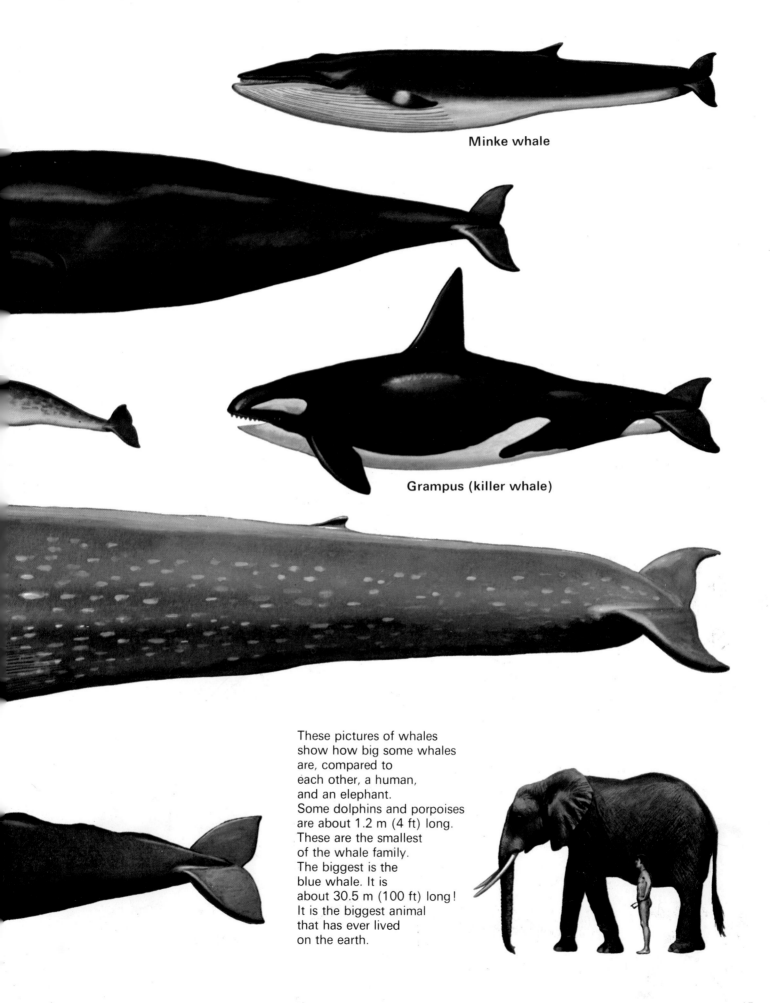

Minke whale

Grampus (killer whale)

These pictures of whales
show how big some whales
are, compared to
each other, a human,
and an elephant.
Some dolphins and porpoises
are about 1.2 m (4 ft) long.
These are the smallest
of the whale family.
The biggest is the
blue whale. It is
about 30.5 m (100 ft) long!
It is the biggest animal
that has ever lived
on the earth.

# Seals and Sea Cows

Seals, sea lions, and walrus, all belong to the seal family. Manatees and dugongs belong to the sea cow family. The pictures show how big some seals and sea cows are, compared to each other, and a human.

The male elephant seal is 6 m (20 ft) long. It is the biggest seal. A manatee is 2.7 m (9 ft) long.

Bearded seal

Elephant seal

Southern sea lion

Common seal

Hooded seal

Harp seal

Manatee (sea cow)

# Stories About Whales

## The whaleship *Essex*

The *Essex* was a wooden whaling ship.
It was an American whaler.
It was hunting whales near the equator,
in the Pacific Ocean,
on November 20, 1820.
A big sperm whale charged the *Essex*,
and smashed some of its planks.
The ship began to sink.
The sailors put bread and water
into three little rowing boats.
There were twenty sailors.
They sailed for a month,
in the three little boats
until they came to a tiny island.
Three men stayed on the island.
The rest sailed toward South America.

A storm drove one boat away
from the other two.
This boat had five men in it.
Two died. A ship saved the other three,
on February 18, 1821.
The other two boats drifted apart,
at the end of January.
One had seven men in it.
No one knows what became of them.
One man died in the last boat,
and then another died. A ship saved
the last two, on February 23, 1821.
Another ship was sent to the island,
for the three men who had stayed there.
This is a true story.

The first officer of the *Essex*
was called Owen Chase.
He was one of the three men
who were saved on February 18.
He wrote a book about his adventures.

Herman Melville was a sailor
who had sailed in a whaler three times.
He read Chase's book, and
wrote a thriller called *Moby Dick*.
Moby Dick was a great sperm whale,
like the real whale who sank the *Essex*.

## James Bartley

This is a whale-hunter's tall story.
The whaler *Star of the East*
was chasing a big sperm whale,
near the Falkland Islands in 1891.
The whale smashed and sank
one of the ship's little wooden boats.
The six sailors from the boat
fell into the sea. Five were saved.
The sixth man was called James Bartley.
No one could find him, so
the other men thought he had drowned.

When the big sperm whale was killed, and
the hunters were cutting up the body,
they saw something moving
in its stomach.
They cut the stomach open, and found—
James Bartley. He was unconscious.
All the bare parts of his body
were bleached quite white.
He woke up at last, but could not
remember much of what had happened.
It is a great pity that
this interesting story isn't true.

# Facts and Figures

## How long do they live?

Whales and seals
live a long life.

Most kinds of seals
live for about 30 years.
Gray seals
and ringed seals
live for about 40 years.

Most female seals
mate and have pups
when they are about
two or three years old.
Male seals don't mate
until they are
about five years old.

The biggest seal
is the elephant seal.
A male can weigh
over 2,000 kg (2 tons).
The heaviest part
is the thick blubber.

Fin whales live
about 90 years.
They mate and have calves
when they are five.

The sperm whale lives
for about 55 years.
The females mate
when they are 10 years old.
Males don't mate
until they're 25 years old.

Sperm whales can dive
to the bottom of the sea.
A sperm whale
killed in 1969
weighed 31,430 kg (31 tons).

A blue whale killed in 1948
weighed 127,540 kg.
This is 125.5 long tons.
The blue whale can be
well over 30.5 m (100 ft) long.

## Safe numbers

Hunters of sea mammals
have to take care
not to kill them all off.
The number of those who die
must be the same as
the number of those born.
This is called the "safe number."

Some kinds of animals
have died out because
of hunting by humans.
Humans can wipe out
families of animals.
We can't bring them back.

Scientists now
help hunters find
the safe number
of sea mammals to catch.
They work out
how many die each year,
and how many are born.

The tables on the left
show the numbers of
four important whales.
Scientists can guess
what was the number
of each kind
before it was hunted.
This is the "original number."
The number of blue whales
is much less than
the safe number.
The fin whale is in danger.
The other two whales
are all right.

**Numbers of whales**

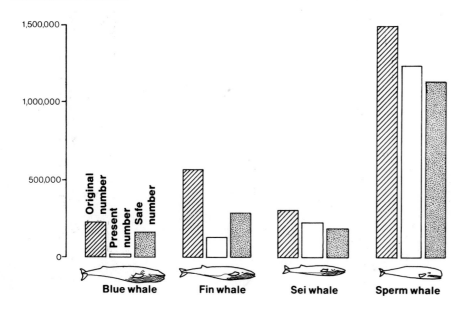

## The International Whaling Commission

This group is in charge
of most of the whaling
done all over the world.
It was set up in 1946, and
15 countries belong to it.

The Commission
tells its members
how many whales
they may catch every year.
It has inspectors see
that no one catches
more than the safe number
of each kind of whale.

## Rules about catching seals

There is no one group
that tells every country
how many seals
may be caught.

Some countries have
their own rules
about this.
These are countries
with seals living
around their coasts.

Nations that catch seals
have special agreements
about how many seals
each may catch.
Before 1911,
each nation caught
as many as it liked.
Today there are many
more seals in the world.

## Marking whales

Scientists mark
whales and seals
to find out their habits.

A dart is fired
into the whale's blubber.
It has a number on it.
It also has the name
of the place
from which it came.
The dart is sent back,
if the whale is killed.

Discs with numbers
are put on seals' flippers.
Some seals with thick fur
can be branded.
Seals can have
tiny radios fixed to them.
The signals from these
tell the scientists
where the seals are.

## Ambergris

This is a lump
of ambergris.
Ambergris is made
in the sperm whale's
intestine.
Ambergris is used
in making perfume.
It holds other scents, also.
It is usually found
in small pieces.

**Whale mark
(real size)**

# Facts and Figures

## Sonar

Whales often dive
when they are hunted.
Sperm whales can stay
under the water
for an hour.
They must come up, then,
to get more air.

Hunters would often lose
a sperm whale
in former times.
They did not know
where it was,
after it had dived.

Look at the picture
below.

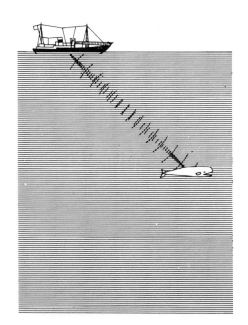

A modern whaler
tracks a whale
with sonar.

The sonar operator
sends down a beam
of high sounds
into the sea.
These sounds bounce back
from the whale's body.
This is an "echo."

Look at page 30.
See how the dolphin
finds a fish by the echo.
The sonar operator
finds the whale
in just the same way.

The sonar beam
follows the whale
as it comes up for air.
The harpoon gun
is put into place,
to shoot the whale
as soon as it is seen.

Moby Dick himself
couldn't have got away
from a modern whaler.

## Whaling and science

Scientists find things out
about whales
in two ways.

They watch tame whales.
These are mostly dolphins
and other small whales.
The biggest tame whale
is the killer whale.
Scientists also study
the ear plugs, bones,
and other parts of
whales killed by hunters.

## Whaling museums

Here are some museums
that deal with whaling:

Whaling Museum
Nantucket, Mass., U.S.A.

Old Dartmouth Historical
Society Whaling Museum
New Bedford, Mass., U.S.A.

Broughty Castle Museum
Dundee, Scotland.

Maritime Museum
Hull, England.

Museum and Art Gallery
Whitby, England.

(The whaler
*Charles W. Morgan*
is kept at Mystic Seaport,
Mystic, Conn., U.S.A.)

# Important Words

**Aquarium**
A tank full of water,
in which fish or
sea mammals live.

**Baleen**
A grid of "whalebone"
that some whales have
instead of teeth.
(See page 16.)

**Blubber**
Thick fat under a whale's
or a seal's skin.
Blubber keeps
the animal warm and
stores its food.

**Breathing hole**
A hole through which
a seal breathes
when it is hunting
under thick ice.
(See page 36.)

**Bull**
A grown-up male whale,
seal, sea lion, or sea cow.

**Calf**
A whale or sea cow
before it grows up.

**Cow**
A grown-up female whale,
seal, sea lion, or sea cow.

**Echo**
A sound that bounces back
from a thing it hits
to the animal or person
that made it.
Sea mammals find food,
and their way,
by using echoes.
Whale hunters also
use echoes, to find
a whale under the water.
(See pages 30, 36, and 52.)

**Flippers**
The hands and feet
of seals, sea lions,
and whales.
They use their flippers
to steer or swim.

**Fur seal**
A seal with a thick coat
and back flippers
for walking.
It is called an "eared seal."
because its ears
can easily be seen.

**Krill**
The name given to shrimps
by whale hunters.
Whales with a baleen
feed on krill.

**Mammal**
An animal that feeds
its babies on its own milk.

**Migration**
A yearly journey
of an animal or bird
between a hot and a cold
part of the world.
(See pages 22 and 23.)

**Molting**
The yearly loss of fur,
so that new fur
may grow in its place.

**Pup**
A seal before it
is grown-up.

**Sea lion**
An "eared seal" with
a thin fur coat
and back flippers
for walking.

**Tail flukes**
The two flat blades
of a whale's tail.

**True seal**
A seal that cannot
walk on its back flippers.
It is called an
"earless seal," because
its ears can't easily
be seen.

# Paper Whale and Walrus

**How to make a paper whale**

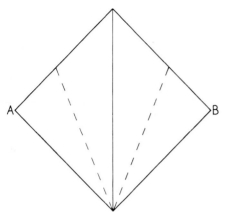

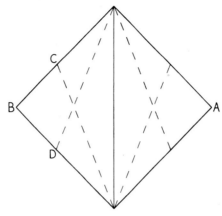

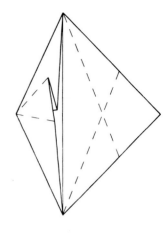

1. Fold A and B to the center line. Open up.

2. Turn paper round and repeat. Fold C and D to center line.

3. Fold along dotted lines so that flap sticks up. Do it again on other side.

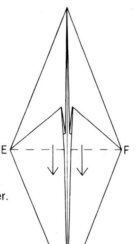

4. Fold flaps down and turn paper over.

5. Fold back E and F to center line, a little below center of the paper. Cut along center line as shown. Fold the top corner over towards you. Fold the body in half towards you, along the center line.

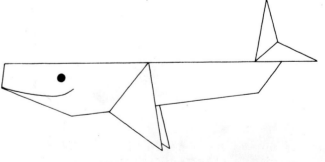

6. Fold back the flipper on each side along the dotted line. Fold the tail upwards along the dotted line. Open up the tail flukes.

7. Draw mouth and eyes.

**How to make a paper walrus**

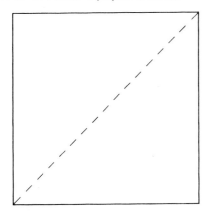

1. Fold paper in half along dotted line.

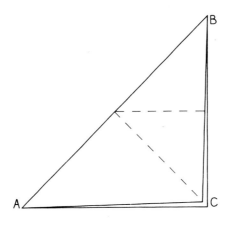

2. Fold A on to B along dotted line. Open up. Fold B on to C along dotted line. Open up.

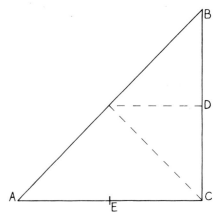

3. Pull down D (single thickness) to E and fold A on to C. Turn over and do the same.

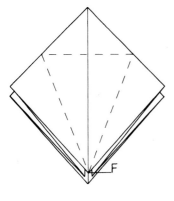

4. Put the square of paper so that the open corners face you. Fold the sides to the middle along the dotted lines. Fold the top over along the dotted line. Open all these up. Pull up flap at F, and press paper back along the creases you have already made.

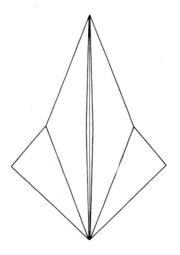

5. Do the same on the other side.

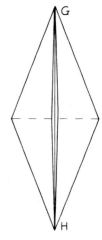

6. Fold top flap along dotted line down to H.

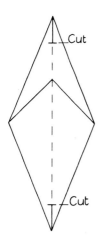

7. Cut where shown and fold the paper in half towards you along the dotted line.

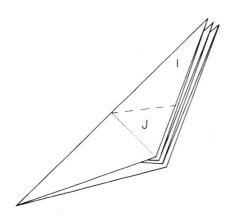

8. Fold I under J along the dotted line. Do the same on other side. Fold hind flippers forward along cut in the same way.

9. Fold inwards along front cut for tusks. Draw the eyes.

# How to Make Whales and Seals

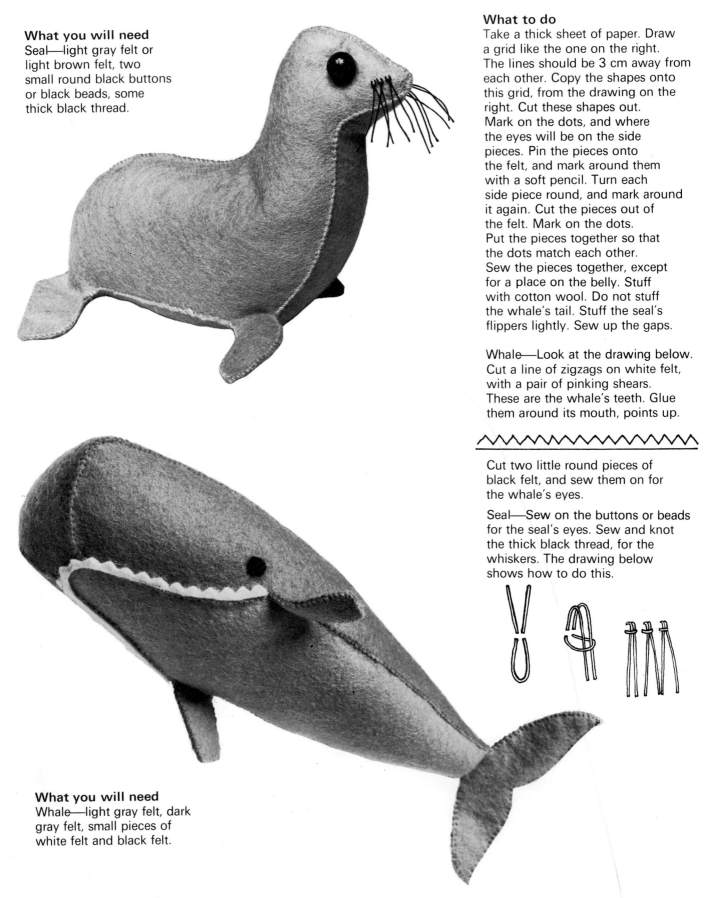

## What you will need

Seal—light gray felt or light brown felt, two small round black buttons or black beads, some thick black thread.

## What to do

Take a thick sheet of paper. Draw a grid like the one on the right. The lines should be 3 cm away from each other. Copy the shapes onto this grid, from the drawing on the right. Cut these shapes out. Mark on the dots, and where the eyes will be on the side pieces. Pin the pieces onto the felt, and mark around them with a soft pencil. Turn each side piece round, and mark around it again. Cut the pieces out of the felt. Mark on the dots. Put the pieces together so that the dots match each other. Sew the pieces together, except for a place on the belly. Stuff with cotton wool. Do not stuff the whale's tail. Stuff the seal's flippers lightly. Sew up the gaps.

Whale—Look at the drawing below. Cut a line of zigzags on white felt, with a pair of pinking shears. These are the whale's teeth. Glue them around its mouth, points up.

Cut two little round pieces of black felt, and sew them on for the whale's eyes.

Seal—Sew on the buttons or beads for the seal's eyes. Sew and knot the thick black thread, for the whiskers. The drawing below shows how to do this.

## What you will need

Whale—light gray felt, dark gray felt, small pieces of white felt and black felt.

56

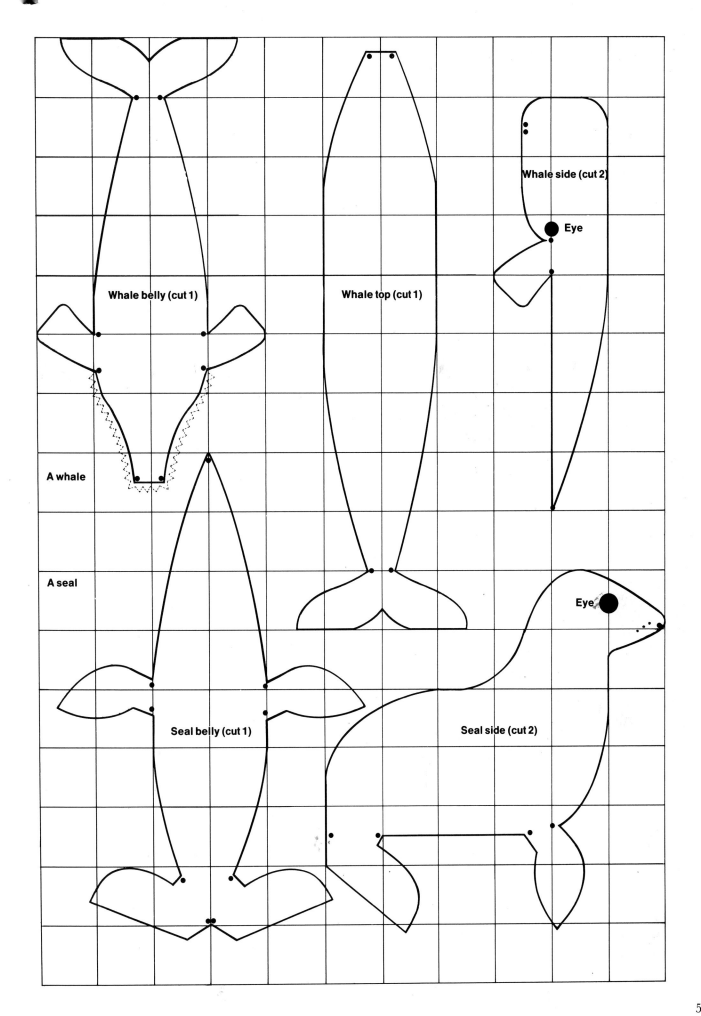

Whale belly (cut 1)

Whale top (cut 1)

Whale side (cut 2)

Eye

A whale

A seal

Seal belly (cut 1)

Seal side (cut 2)

Eye

# How to Draw Whales and Seals

**Drawing a seal**

1. Draw three oval shapes, as above.

2. Draw flippers and tail, as above.

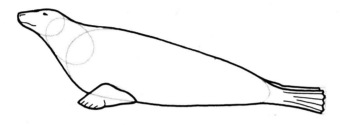

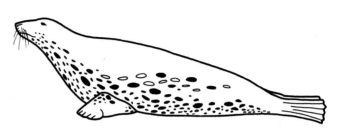

3. Draw a thick line around these shapes. Draw the eyes and mouth.

4. Draw the whiskers, and spots on the skin.

**Drawing a dolphin**

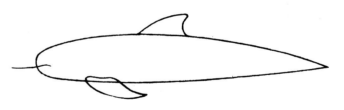

1. Draw a long shape, with one round and one pointed end.

2. Draw a fin and flipper. Draw a line for the mouth.

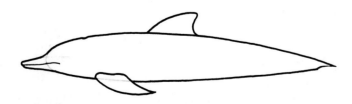

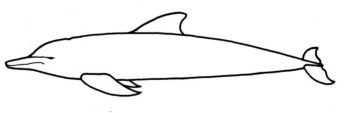

3. Draw a thick line around these shapes. Draw the beak.

4. Draw the tail and the second flipper.

**Drawing a baleen whale**

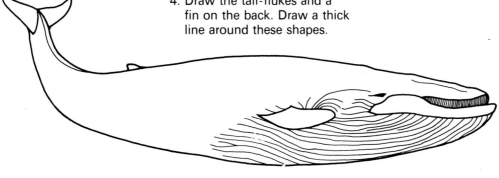

1. Draw a long shape. Start it at the tail.

2. Draw mouth, eye, and flipper.

3. Draw the tail. Fill in the mouth.

4. Draw the tail-flukes and a fin on the back. Draw a thick line around these shapes.

5. Draw the baleen. Draw the grooves on the skin.

# Index to Pictures and Text

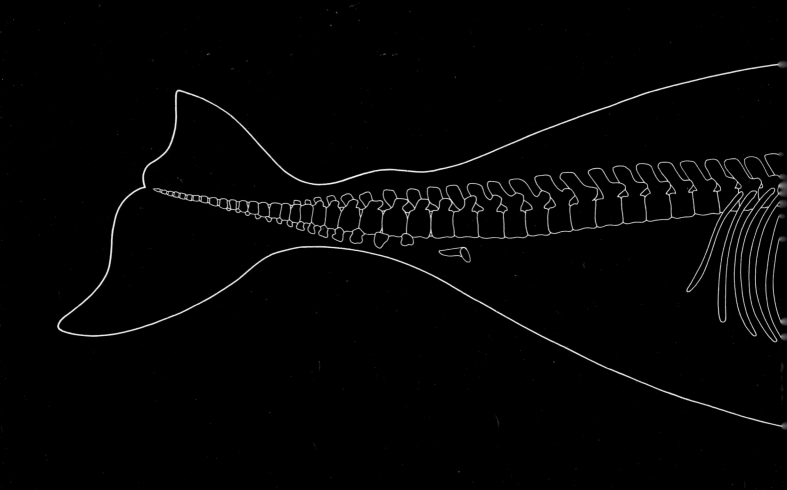

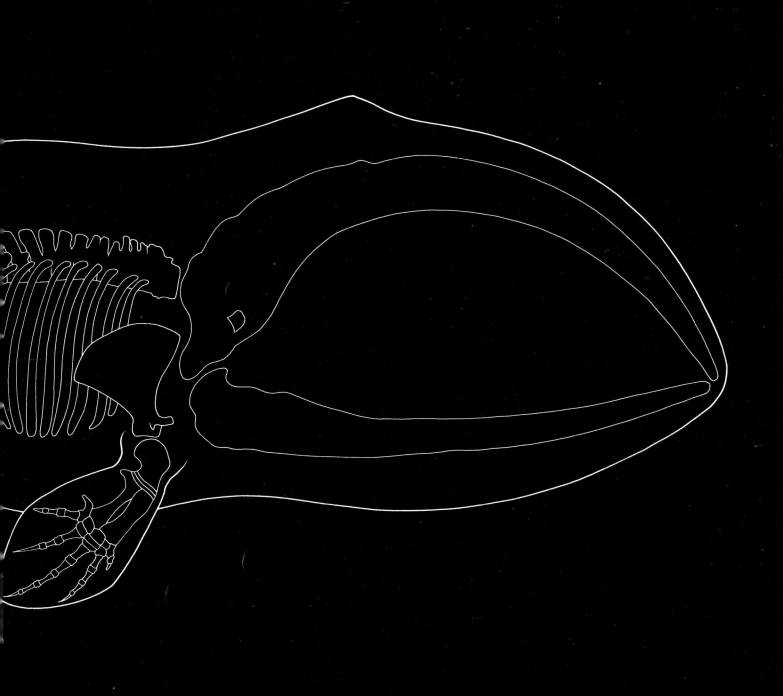

1 2 3 4 5 6 7 8 9  Cad  84 83 82 81 80 79